For car sales, real estate and lending professionals

Generate more sales, higher approvals, more commissions

Step by step quick guide for repairing your client's credit on the spot

3 free websites to obtain credit bureau reports.
1. www.creditkarma.com
2. www.freecreditreport.com
3. www.annualcreditreport.com

Directly

Equifax 1-800-685-1111
TransUnion 1-800-888-4213
Experian 1-888-397-3742

Experian
P.O. Box 4500
Allen, TX 75013

Equifax Credit Information Services, Inc.
P.O. Box 740256
Atlanta, GA 30374
TransUnion, LLC
P.O. Box 2000
Chester, PA 19022

First step!! Dispute all personal information that is not your current address and employer. Call in to the credit bureau call center and do this BEFORE starting any paper disputes. Tell them to please remove ABC address and or employer. The information is inaccurate. This will usually update in 48hrs. This is vital because if an OLD account can be linked to any address on your credit report it will come back
"verified".

NEXT

Always use a copy of the clients DL & SSN card and utility bill include the words for verification of identity.

Enlarge the Drivers License in COLOR.

Make sure the address of the DL and utility bill are the same.

Hand write all disputes

5 disputes per letter, mail different days

Use certified mail delivery to have verification of the date the bureau signed for your letter. They have exactly 30 days from the date of this letter to correct, validate and investigate your disputes or they must be deleted.

Look for all old negative accounts past 7 years

Look for any accounts breaking new credit laws

Look for any accounts with missing information, and missing payment history

Look for any accounts that are negative and paid

Look for Judgments & Bankruptcies court fling dates and amounts dispute

Look for account with joint   owners dispute as not original owner

Remove authorized users

Any collection that has been sent back to the original creditor must be removed

Call the collector and see when the account will be returned to the original creditor

Check the state Statute of Limitations, do not have to pay if it has expired

Look for any collections that have not been updated in the past 6 months " collection agencies must reconcile collections that have not been paid in full. Collection accounts that have not been updated in the past 6 months must be deleted.

Look for paid medical collections, credit bureaus must remove
Send debt validation letters to collection agencies who are recent and may not have much to dispute

Send disputes during holidays

Look for late payments over 3 years old on closed accounts

Write directly to the creditor to remove "paid" collections

Never do disputes via the credit bureaus online system

For better results get it notarized and send it certified

Write a letter to cease and desist b/c the debt has legally expired

Medical debt Medical dated sooner than 180? The new 2015 credit law states that medical debt won't be reported until after 180- day waiting period to allow time for insurance payments to be applied. The credit reporting agencies agreed to remove from credit reports previously reported medical collections that have been or are being paid by insurance companies.

Parking tickets, library late fees, and similar fines should no longer appear on consumer credit reports. If the debt did not arise from an agreement to pay it should be disputed with a request to delete.

If a collection agency has not updated a collection account in the prior 6 months please dispute with the request to remove or suppress due to lack of activity for 6 months. This account has not been reconciled or updated in the past 6 months. Please remove or suppress.

The credit bureaus use a system called OCR, Optical Character Recognition. If they see the same letter used in the past, they will give your file a red flag and your disputes won't get anywhere.

Look for repeated **CO CO** codes in your credit report when they are reporting of charge offs

The status of charge off is correct BUT it's the DATE of the original charge off that's incorrect. It continues to reflect as a current occurrence when it only happened once. It cannot continue to "happen" every 30 days. So one must check the "date of" status and dispute it directly with the creditor because if its disputed with the bureau I know Experian just updates automatically the "date of "status to the dispute date which ruins the credit score.

Provide the creditor with the definition of charge off, and a copy of the credit report showing a charge off happening every 30 days and then insist they update the reporting

Bankruptcy- Have your attorney request to have your file checked out. File your dispute, they have 30 days to verify. If your information cannot be found then the credit bureaus must delete.

You are **judgment** proof if you are

- Unemployed
- Retired
- Have no money or assets

If a creditor or collection agency attempts to sue and you are judgment proof then respond to the judgment and say so.

Motion to vacate a **judgment**- Ask an attorney to file a motion of Process for the purpose of having the judgment removed from your credit file. Have the attorney argue that the file was not served properly. The creditor must appear in court with an attorney to prove the initial legal process was done properly.

When disputing any government liens, bankruptcies, judgments ect. Input the case/ file number where the account number would go.

Never request old credit accounts be deleted. Deleting old credit accounts HURT your credit score and file. Only dispute negative information.

Pay all open credit cards down to where they are 30% balance. If you insist on paying off your accounts then pay them but do not close them. Paying and closing will not increase a score. The number of good standing accounts that have been used and opened the longest is what is best.

Ask your creditor for a 1099-c Cancellation of Debt – the debt must be over $600

When a lender cancels your debt, you may have to report this as taxable income on your federal income taxes, unless there is an exception. If you're required to report the cancelled debt, the lender will send IRS Form 1099-C to you.

Debt Validation from a debt collection agency only. They must provide the following

- Proof that the collection agency owns the debt, has been assigned the debt
- Account statements from the original creditor, complete payment history
- Copy of original signed loan agreement or credit card application
- FDCPA Section 809 Validation of debts { 15 USC 1692g}

If the collector cannot validate the debt then

- They are not allowed to collect the debt
- They are not allowed to contact you about the debt
- They are not allowed to report it under FCRA
- Continuing to report is a violation and you can sue for $1000 per violation

- If they reply with a summons to sue cite that they cannot even sue without validating a debt within the 30 day period. Cite the case Spears vs. Brennan. They cannot get a judgment without satisfying the FDCPA law.
- Contact the credit bureaus and mail proof that the collectors did not verify the debt.

For criminal records obtain the form called " **Motion and Order for Expungement of Conviction or**
Diversion and Related Arrest Records. You may have to hire a lawyer or do it pro se in your local
Municipal court. Request an **Order for Expungement**

Master dispute reasons

- Information not based on my identity
- Information is outdated and resolved
- The time limit on the information has occurred
- The account type is inaccurate
- The incorrect balance is being reported
- The date the account opened is incorrect
- The terms are incorrect that's being reported
- This is an obsolete account
- This account was transferred to another lender- It is a LAW that once a collector sells a debt to another collector or sends it back to the original creditor they are required to remove the account from my credit report.
- The account designation is incorrect
- The late pays are inaccurate
- The original creditor is not listed
- This account belongs to another individual with a similar name
- I am not aware of this collection
- A settlement or partial payment was accepted on this
- This was late due to a change of address, I never received the statement
- The credit limits are incorrect
- This account is included in the bankruptcy of another person
- This account is closed
- I am or was in active military duty
- An insurance claim was delayed on this
- I was a victim of a natural or declared disaster
- I am not liable for this account it belongs to (ex spouse, business ect…)
- This account was fraudulently opened

- Fraudulent charges were made on this account
- The dates of the last payment, open date, payment rating, payment history are incorrect
- The current balance, original loan amount, scheduled monthly payment amount is incorrect
- The company promised they would be changing or deleting this
- This account is not mine
- This debt did not arise from a contract or agreement to pay
- This collection agency is past the six month allotted collection time
- This medical collection has been paid
- Wrong credit limit
- Duplicate reporting
- Closed account showing as open
- Charged off account showing a balance
- Inaccurate account number
- Inaccurate account name
- Inaccurate creditor address
- Inaccurate payment received
- Inaccurate credit limit
- Inaccurate date closed
- Accounts are unverifiable
- The original creditor is wrong
- The account is erroneous

Letter Writing

At the top of each letter include the following
1. Your name
2. Social Security Number
3. Date of Birth
4. Address
5. Name and address of the credit Bureau you are writing

Use the following format for each dispute. Do this for EACH dispute

- Today's Date
- Name of creditor
- Account Number
- Dollar amount of account
- Dispute Reason
- What you want done – Deleted, Updated, Removed, Corrected

In the BODY of each letter include a short, simple, easy to read request letter.

Sample

I have reviewed my credit file and noticed that it contains errors and incomplete information. I am very distraught over this misinformation. I have listed each item below that needs correction. Please review these accounts, delete or update them and reply with a corrected credit report file within 30 days. For your verification of identity I have enclosed an enlarged copy of my driver's license and recent utility bill.

CC: Federal Trade Commission, State Attorney General

Include **CC** at the end of your letters Carbon Copy. This lets the bureaus know that these other agencies are receiving copies of your letter as well. They will pay extra care when handling your dispute.

For **inquiry** removals use the BODY below

Your company is reporting INQUIRIES that are the result of fraudulent activities. It must be noted that I did not apply for credit accounts with the below listed companies and creditors, some of these are the result of attempts to open accounts, but the companies did not approve these accounts. Therefore, these inquiries must be deleted from within my credit file. You cannot delete the fraudulently opened accounts without also deleting the fraudulent inquiries. It should be noted that an inquiry that was not made by me is not a factual record, just as a fraudulently opened account is not a factual record and not referred to the creditor to be disputed directly with them. The credit reporting agencies have attempted to address an inquiry as a factual record of file access, but if it was done through fraudulent means, it is not a factual record. As a consumer I should not be required to dispute each fraudulent inquiry directly with each company. These inquiries are the result of fraudulent activity and therefore inaccurate information in which the credit reporting agencies or the creditors cannot verify, meaning that these inquiries are unverifiable information and must be deleted from out of my credit file.

Follow up dispute letter body.
Sample

Dear credit bureau,

This is the second letter requesting that you make corrections to my credit file. It seems to me that you are refusing to investigate my disputes which is a violation of the FCRA. Because of your noncompliance I am forced to file complaints with the FDIC, and the Comptroller of the Currency Federal reserve System. For the 2nd time please investigate and make the needed corrections to my disputes.

Follow up final letter body sample

It is now my 3rd letter and your company has still refused to investigate the incomplete and misleading information that you are reporting. Because of your failures I have lost the opportunity to obtain a home and a job for me and my children. My credit worthiness and character are both damaged. Therefore I have to seek legal advice if the below accounts are not fixed.

Statute of Limitations Guide

Making a partial or any payment at all on an old account will restart the 7 year clock on credit bureau reporting!

What is a statute of limitations? The time limit a state gives that lets you know a debt is legally expired. After this time you cannot be sued and the debt cannot be legally enforced. It does not dismiss the debt, they can still keep it on your credit report. No SOL for state taxes. Tax liens are collectible for 6-10 yrs

State	Written	Oral	Open-ended Accounts
Alabama	3	6	3
Alaska	3	6	3
Arizona	6	3	3
Arkansas	5	3	5
California	4	2	4
Colorado	6	6	6
Connecticut	6	3	6
Delaware	3	3	3
D.C.	3	3	3
Florida	5	4	4
Georgia	6	4	4 or 6
Hawaii	6	6	6
Idaho	5	4	5
Illinois	10	5	5 or 10
Indiana	10	6	6
Iowa	10	5	10
Kansas	3	3	3
Kentucky	15	5	5 or 15
Louisiana	3	10	3
Maine	6	6	6
Maryland	3	3	3
Massachusetts	6	6	6
Michigan	6	6	6
Minnesota	6	6	6
Mississippi	3	3	3
Missouri	5	5	5
Montana	8	5	8
Nebraska	4	4	4

Nevada	4	4	4
New Hampshire	3	3	3
New Jersey	6	6	6
New Mexico	4	4	4
New York	6	6	6
North Carolina	3	3	3
North Dakota	6	6	6
Ohio	6	6	6
Oklahoma	5	3	3 or 5
Oregon	6	6	6
Pennsylvania	4	4	4
Rhode Island	10	10	10
South Carolina	10	10	3
South Dakota	6	3	6
Tennessee	6	6	6
Texas	4	4	4
Utah	6	4	4
Vermont	5	3	3
Virginia	6	6	6
Washington	6	3	6
West Virginia	10	10	10
Wisconsin	6	6	6
Wyoming	10	8	8

Chexsystems Quick Guide

For individuals who are barred from obtaining a traditional checking account due to being in
Chexsystems do the following

- Visitwww.chexhelp.com to order a copy of your chexsystems report
- Chexsystems Customer Service

  12005 Ford Rd, Suite 600 Dallas TX 75234-7253

  #1800-428-9623 or 800-513-7125

- Dispute any inaccurate information just as you would a credit bureau, mail the dispute certified mail along with your ID and utility bill
- Keep a copy for your records
- Look specifically for anything they omitted or left blank and dispute that needs to be verified and that it is incomplete

DELETED

DELETED

DELETED